Living With OCD

BY JEFFREY POWELL

A Powerful Guide To Understanding Obsessive Compulsive Disorder in Children And Adults

2nd Edition

Table Of Contents

Introduction

I want to thank you and congratulate you for purchasing the book, *"Living with OCD: A Powerful Guide to Understanding Obsessive Compulsive Disorder in Children and Adults."*

This book contains proven steps and strategies on how to better understand obsessive compulsive disorder (OCD) and how to cope with it.

Obsessive compulsive disorder is quite a common thing that plagues a lot of people today. It is not an isolated case. You or your loved ones may have it as well. Knowing what you are up against can help you get better equipped for fighting this debilitating battle against your thoughts and actions. In this book, you will learn what obsessive compulsive disorder is, how it differs from a similarly named disorder called obsessive compulsive personality disorder (OCPD), how obsessive compulsive disorder affects adults and children, and what you can do to remove or at least lessen the torment caused by it.

Thanks again for purchasing this book, I hope you enjoy it!

Chapter 1 – What Is OCD?

First of all, you have to know *what* you are dealing with before you can determine *how* you can deal with it. So the very first question that will be answered is: What is OCD?

OCD or obsessive compulsive disorder is a debilitating anxiety disorder that is evident of uncontrollable thoughts (obsessions) that intrude the mind and make the sufferer feel uneasy, apprehensive, fearful, or worrisome. It is also characterized by repetitive actions (compulsions) that are done to alleviate the unpleasant feelings mentioned above. Most of the time, both obsessions and compulsions are present in the sufferer at the same time.

OBSESSIONS

On the other hand, examples of the obsessions include an extreme preoccupation with thoughts that are sexually-oriented, thoughts that are violent or macabre, thoughts that are religiously blasphemous, intense aversion to specific numbers or letters, and basically any uninvited and intrusive thought that permeates your consciousness and subconscious that it almost seems like paranoia or psychosis and resists your efforts to ignore or control them. It can either be a vague or vivid thought.

It can range from preoccupation with little details or events to absolute madness. A person may feel a general sense of tension or a feeling similar to being adrift at sea with no oar or sail or rudder, a feeling that can be debilitating. A person may also be preoccupied with thoughts of someone the sufferer knows or cares about dying or being killed or harmed.

Others have obsessive thoughts of a sexual nature. A person's mind may be filled with thoughts and images of sexual acts such as kissing, fondling, caressing, oral sex, anal sex, vaginal penetration, homosexual acts, rape, masturbation, or incest involving persons the sufferer may or may not know or may or may not be close to, and in some cases, sexual acts with, or of animals.

Indeed, people who do not suffer from obsessive compulsive disorder may also have sexual thoughts that intrude their minds. However, a person who suffers from obsessive compulsive disorder attaches more than the usual significance to those sexual thoughts. The thoughts and images, especially if they are of homosexual orientation, may lead to excessive fears about the sufferer's sexual identity that he may indeed be homosexual because of having homosexual thoughts or be a pedophile if the obsessions include sex with children. Moreover, these thoughts can be so great that the sufferer may be compelled to act on such thoughts that will result in criticizing or self-loathing.

There is also what is called "Pure-O" or purely obsessive disorder characterized by having the intrusive thoughts or obsessions without the compulsive actions that commonly accompany the thoughts. People suffering from purely obsessional OCD have distressing and intrusive thoughts suddenly popping up their minds frequently and at times when the sufferer's original train of thought was not at all related in any way to the intrusive thoughts.

Rather than acting on the unwanted, intrusive thoughts, purely obsessional sufferers resort to either mental rituals or avoidance. If they choose to avoid the situations where the thoughts are more likely to pop up, they may appear irresponsible, especially if they are asked to perform a certain role or responsibility during those situations. The sufferer's avoidance often causes confusion and/or frustration for other people, especially if they do not know the reason for the evasiveness.

On the other hand, if they resort to mental rituals, it consumes so much time that should otherwise be used for more important activities. Instead of performing tasks for the day, the sufferer may spend so much time trying to control his uncontrollable thoughts. He would be spending much of his waking hours trying to organize and de-clutter his thoughts leading to decreased productivity and causing other people to think that the sufferer is lazy or procrastinating on purpose to avoid working.

COMPULSIONS

Compulsions are rituals performed by a person for the reason that they have an inexplicable urge to do it to relieve them of the anxieties caused by their intrusive thoughts. The sufferer feels that by performing certain rituals will somehow prevent a fear from coming true, or it takes their mind off the anxiety they feel about certain things. The sufferer's reasoning behind their compulsions are usually without sense or is distorted, which results to frustration on the side of the sufferer and on those whom the sufferer interacts with, especially family members living together with the sufferer.

Examples of these compulsions include washing of the hands repeatedly, cleaning of the house every hour or so, constantly checking if doors are locked, repeatedly checking if the stove or oven is turned off, or being compelled to buy or hoard items (sometimes much more than what their homes can accommodate).

It can also be evident in a person's manner of doing things, like counting footsteps, looking for certain patterns or certain intervals or symmetry, doing repetitive actions, or having the urge to follow the same routine every day. However, doing something repeatedly does not automatically qualify as a compulsion. Reading every night before bedtime is not a compulsion if it is done for the purpose of learning or relaxation. An act only qualifies as a compulsion if it disrupts everyday life instead of enriching it.

It oftentimes makes others feel repulsed by a sufferer's behavior since it can be frustrating to watch someone do things over and over again in excess of what is proper, normal, or enough. Moreover, since it is done repeatedly instead of just once or twice, it uses up much more time to accomplish and can infuriate others who are waiting for the sufferer to finish. To the sufferer himself, it also causes frustrations on his part because aside from the compulsions and rituals being time-consuming, they are also emotionally and financially draining.

Chapter 2 – OCD or OCPD?

Since obsessive compulsive disorder is quite common, it is also common to hear "OC" used as an adjective to describe people who are very meticulous, who are perfectionists, controlling, absorbed, or intensely focused. Although those traits are visible in obsessive compulsive disorder, it is not automatic that a person who has them really has obsessive compulsive disorder. Instead, they may be suffering from another type of anxiety disorder.

One of those anxiety disorders which highly resemble obsessive compulsive disorder is obsessive compulsive *personality* disorder. However, there is a difference between the two.

Obsessive compulsive personality disorder is characterized by excessive pursuit of order, perfection, control, and power, which causes great stress and suffering on the individual and the people who have a relationship with the individual. Persons with obsessive compulsive disorder are not satisfied with a half-hearted job or even an accomplished or completed job that does not live up to the sufferer's standard of accomplishment or completion.

The sufferer has difficulty relaxing or just taking things slow because they always have the urge to do and accomplish things before time runs out on them, supposedly. This creates unnecessary stress for the sufferer because he does not take time out to relax or unwind. They see to it that when a job needs to be done, it will be done on time and in the most perfect way possible.

Sufferers also show excessive regard for orderliness, perfection, and control when they plan activities or events. When the responsibility of planning an activity or event falls on the sufferer's shoulders, he would plan it down to the last and smallest detail. For example, when making an itinerary for a trip, a person with obsessive compulsive personality disorder would plan every single thing that every single person will do, eat, or go to. Anything unpredictable or unexpected will surely upset the person with obsessive compulsive personality disorder because they feel that allowing it will result in loss of control.

The most prominent symptom that people with obsessive compulsive personality disorder has is the obsession with cleanliness or cleaning. Daily living becomes more difficult for them because they would spend an awful lot of time cleaning and tidying up until they achieve their own standard of cleanliness and order.

Also, persons with obsessive compulsive personality disorder have a certain rigidity when it comes to their own or to others' beliefs and actions. Sufferers tend to classify actions and beliefs into two polarities only with no middle ground. It can only be "right" or "wrong". This creates a strain between a sufferer and the people who live with or who have a relationship with the sufferer.

This strain on their relationships causes either of two things. The sufferer can either resort to anger or violence when they do not see eye to eye about things or the sufferer may wallow in self-pity because of being misunderstood and resort to suicidal attempts.

Having obsessive compulsive personality disorder can be a good thing because of the intense attention to detail and perfection. People with obsessive compulsive personality disorder can do great at checking and correcting things. They can be great editors and proofreaders in publishing companies. They would do greatly in accomplishing tasks within the frame of time they are assigned to work in.

Their strict adherence to rules, orders, regulations, and schedules can make them very good law enforcers or lawyers as their employers or clients can rest assured that they will be doing their very best to uphold the law and regulations of any institution or company they are working for.

However, their being perfectionists can also be a boon to their job. Other times, their perfectionism would hinder them from completing a task because the output does not or cannot conform to the sufferer's standard of perfection. Moreover, because they only want their own standards to be met, they often refuse to delegate tasks to other people because they do not trust them to do things exactly the way the sufferer wants things to be done, and this kind of behavior can create strain within the work place.

Their extreme devotion to their work, while beneficial for their employer, is a cause for discord within the family and the friends of the sufferer because the time that should be spent with the family or with friends are all funneled into accomplishing the sufferer's work or project. In their relationships, a sufferer's rigidity in moral or ethical matters as evidenced by being overly conscientious or stubborn may also cause strain when dealing with people.

The causes of obsessive compulsive personality disorder can be either hereditary or environmental. Males are more at risk of inheriting the OCPD gene. However, the genes usually remain dormant for some time until it gets triggered by traumatic physical or psychological events. Even without the OCPD gene, being around people with obsessive compulsive personality disorder for years and years can greatly influence a person to develop it as well.

It might seem that obsessive compulsive disorder and obsessive compulsive personality disorder are exactly the same. However, the two are very distinct disorders. The difference lies in their compulsions and the satisfaction or pleasure they get from performing their compulsions.

Persons with obsessive compulsive disorder act on their obsessions and are greatly urged to perform their rituals repeatedly. On the other hand, persons with obsessive compulsive personality disorder do not feel the need or the urge to perform certain rituals over and over.

In addition, persons with obsessive compulsive disorder are more and more troubled with their actions the more they act on their compulsions, while persons with obsessive compulsive personality disorder feel a sense of accomplishment and relief when they are able to perform their compulsions to the degree of perfection that they want.

Chapter 3 – OCD in Children

For adults, it is hard enough to struggle with obsessive compulsive disorder. One can only imagine how harder it is for children to struggle with the disorder.

SIGNS AND SYMPTOMS

Children who have obsessive compulsive disorder are plagued with thoughts about things that might harm them, that might be dangerous for them, that might be wrong, or unclean. They may also worry about misplacing their things or even losing them, and this is evident in their trying to put everything in order and in their proper place.

Children suffering from obsessive compulsive disorder may have a hard time explaining why they do things repeatedly or in a certain way all the time. The parents will be likely to get a "just because" answer so they need to be especially perceptive and discerning of their child's behavior and habits.

Just like in adults, the children themselves realize the irrationality of repeating certain acts over and over. However, their anxieties get the best of them and the only way that they can feel relief is by performing their rituals or actin on their compulsions.

Indeed, obsessive compulsive disorder can really make everyday life hard for children and adults alike. It not only affects themselves but others as well, especially their family and friends who are close to them. The disorder can cause parents to lose their temper many times in frustration when their child acts on the compulsions, which are most of the time using up much time and energy making relatively easy tasks in the home such as cleaning, tidying up, and other chores more difficult and thus robbing the child of the ability to just enjoy his childhood.

Low self-esteem or doubting oneself is often a problem for children with obsessive compulsive disorder as well. The intrusive thoughts and images in their minds of perceived or imagined dangers or fears and their compulsions to repeatedly behave or do things a certain way when they know that their acting on their obsessions cannot really prevent certain things from happening or that acting on their intrusive thoughts will provide relief from their severe anxiety.

However, obsessive compulsive disorder can be difficult to recognize in children because they can be very good at hiding their compulsions or rituals, especially when they are aware that their compulsions or rituals are irrational or unusual for them to have at their age. It is not surprising to find out that a child has been engaging in repeated actions many months or years before the parents actually know or discern that their child has obsessive compulsive disorder.

In addition, children may not perform such rituals outside the home, which might lead parents to think that their child's behavior is just a normal phase that children go through on their way to their teenage years and into adulthood, and it can indeed be just a phase so parents need to be extra discerning about this.

A child with obsessive compulsive disorder will try to contain the thoughts and images within their minds and not act on them. However, these will build anxiety upon them and they may conclude that they might be going crazy forcing them to hide it even more and try and incorporate their rituals and behaviors into their normal day to day routines and activities so that hopefully no one would notice until they get to the point that they really cannot hide or control it anymore.

It is completely normal for a child to worry about touching something dirty or getting germs on them when the parents have taught their children to keep away from dirty or potentially harmful things. However, when the child starts to obsess and excessively worry about it, then it becomes a thing to be wary about, especially when the child throws tantrums when he is prevented from doing his rituals.

CAUSES

Like what was discussed in the previous chapter, obsessive compulsive disorder shows evidence that it can indeed be passed on from parent to child and the onset of the disorder may start to be visibly evident early on in a child's life, especially when it is triggered by traumatic events or by the influences of people around the child who are also suffering from obsessive compulsive disorder. However, it does not necessarily follow that if a person has the OCD gene in his blood, he will definitely develop OCD. It just means that the person will have a higher probability than most to develop it.

According to experts, it is very likely that the obsessive compulsive disorder can also be caused by blockage in the flow of serotonin to the brain. Serotonin is a chemical that carries electrical signals to the brain. When the serotonin is blocked, the brain reacts excessively and misinterprets the signals as warnings of danger. This in turn will cause the sufferer to do certain things to qualm the warnings of danger from his brain.

It is indeed very important to remember and understand that a child who has obsessive compulsive disorder cannot simply stop having the disorder simply by trying harder to control it. Remember that obsessive compulsive disorder is exactly that—a disorder. And like all disorders of the physical kind, such as asthma, it is not a thing that children can control or cause to develop.

Likewise, parents must remember that obsessive compulsive disorder is also not a thing that they themselves caused to happen to their children. However, as we have discussed, the parents' own behavior or even the normal events in a child's life as he grows up may trigger the development of the disorder in a child who is predisposed to it or may worsen the disorder in a child who has already developed it.

DIAGNOSIS

Although obsessive compulsive disorder is very common in children, it often goes by undiagnosed because of their efforts to hide the compulsions or rituals from the people around them like their parents, their siblings, their friends, their teachers, and others mostly for the reason of feeling ashamed or embarrassed of their behavior because they know that their compulsions are "not normal".

Other times, the signs and symptoms are readily seen and the child does not make efforts to hide his behavior. However, it is the parents who fail to see because of their lack of discernment and perceptiveness of their child. Even health care providers may also miss detecting obsessive compulsive disorder in children because their rituals or tantrums may almost always be attributed to kids "just being kids".

Therefore, parents and doctors alike should be able to tell if the child's behavior or actions use up more than an hour to do every day, if performing the rituals causes distress to the child instead of satisfaction, and if it interferes with the child's normal daily activities and chores.

Diagnosis of obsessive compulsive disorder usually takes place when the child reaches the age of 7 up until right before he enters his teenage years because this is the time when children try to fit in with the rest of his peers and it is during these years when any signs of obsessive compulsive disorder will be clearly evident.

It is beneficial for parents to be proactive instead of being just being reactive. It will be helpful to ask the child questions that will help the parent and the child himself to be able to realize if he has obsessive compulsive disorder or not. Some of these questions can be:

Are you always checking things repeatedly, like opening and closing the door many times to make sure it is closed?

Do you feel that things should be done always in a specific way?

Are you washing your hands a lot even when you just washed them?

Do you always think about bad things that might happen to you or to the people you love?

Are you always worried that something bad might happen?

After asking a question and the child says yes to it, a parent should always follow up with the question, "How many times do you do or feel it?" Even children without obsessive compulsive disorder may say yes to the questions above. However, it is the frequency of it that draws the line between what is considered a normal concern and an obsessive compulsive disorder.

So now that you have an understanding of the disorder, what it is, what causes it, and how you can detect it, the next chapter will discuss the different ways to treat or cope with obsessive compulsive disorder.

Chapter 4 – How to Cope with OCD

There are many ways obsessive compulsive disorder can be treated. The most common and most successful treatment is behavioral therapy (also known as cognitive behavior therapy or CBT) and medication. In children and teenagers most especially, cognitive behavior therapy is the most recommended and most successful treatment for obsessive compulsive disorder.

COGNITIVE BEHAVIOR THERAPY In cognitive behavior therapy, the children are exposed to the very things that they are afraid of or are anxious about. However, the child is instructed not to act on those thoughts and instead recognize that his fears and anxieties will not be realized even if he does nothing about it or at the very least, the fears and anxieties that he has will eventually decrease in intensity.

For this therapy to be a success, the child's compulsions or rituals or his avoidance of them must be blocked. As an example, if the child's fear or anxiousness is of dirt and germs, the child must stay in contact with the object that he deems dirty and will be prevented from washing repeatedly.

In addition, the child needs to feel and know that he is the "boss" of his disorder. Giving the disorder a bad nickname can help the child view it as something that he should not give in to or listen to so that whenever he would get the intrusive thoughts that would cause him to be anxious, he would not act on them and will use his will power to try and control how he views or feels about the anxieties he has.

Like the example given above about a child that is adversely repulsed by dirty things, he will gain confidence in himself when he becomes successful in fighting the urge to wash his hands repeatedly until the urge gradually disappears from his life. However, the parent must remember to keep the therapy consistent and logical and that the parent must be fully supportive of their child, which will give the child more confidence to fight against his disorder.

In addition, different children will have different treatment and recovery duration. Some may break free from the grasp of obsessive compulsive disorder quite speedily compared to other children so a parent needs to exercise patience if the child's response is quite slow. The more the child feels that his parents will support him every step of the way, the more the child will be inclined and motivated to fight his compulsions and obsessions.

MEDICATION

When the symptoms of the obsessive compulsive disorder have proven to be moderate to severe, medicines can be relied on to help with the treatment. If used in conjunction with the cognitive behavior therapy, treatment and recovery will take effect much faster.

Since obsessive compulsive disorder can be caused by the blockage of the serotonin to the brain, antidepressants (usually referred to as SSRI's or Selective Serotonin-Reuptake Inhibitors) will be the first type of medicine that would be prescribed by the doctor.

However, it must be known that medicines can only control

and decrease the symptoms of obsessive compulsive disorder. It does not remove the disorder itself and especially when the disorder is severe, the symptoms can often come back again if the sufferer stops taking the medication.

Moreover, treatment of obsessive compulsive disorder using medication does not happen overnight because all medicines formulated for obsessive compulsive disorder work slowly. A sufferer should not give up right away if he does not see or feel any changes or improvement after a couple of days. The medicine should be taken at the right dosage for at least 10 to 12 weeks before concluding that the medicine is not working.

As with all kinds of medicines though, OCD medications can have some side effects including nausea, restlessness, drowsiness, insomnia, hyperactivity, problems when urinating, gaining of weight, problems with concentration, palpitations, or dryness of the mouth. Therefore, the benefits of the medicine should be weighed against the side effects before continuing on taking the medicine.

More importantly, the sufferer should know that he does not have to put up with the first medicine he was prescribed with if it fails to work on him. Another kind of medicine should be tried, maybe more. Plus, it is still best to pair the taking of medicine with cognitive behavior therapy to get the most out of the treatment.

If the obsessive compulsive disorder is mild to moderate, then the sufferer can survive and cope with the disorder on cognitive behavior therapy alone. However, if it is on the more severe side of things, then the sufferer may continue to need to take medicines to ward off the symptoms since the symptoms can come back after a few weeks or months if the taking of the medicine is stopped.

COMMON MEDICINES THAT HELP TREAT OCD

Many drugs are well-known to help OCD and most of them are antidepressants. According to studies, eight common medicines have been proven effective in reducing symptoms of OCD. These include fluoxetine (Prozac), fluvoxamine (Luvox), paroxetine (Paxil), sertraline (Zoloft), clomipramine (Anafranil), citalopram (Celexa), venlafaxine (Effexor), and escitalopram (Lexapro).

Anfranil is the best studied among these medicines and has been around for many years. According to studies, the other drugs are likewise effective although most of them are new. Furthermore, these drugs have been studied carefully and proven to be very helpful in treating OCD. For instance, duloxetine has been found to be helpful in OCD patients who failed to respond to the other drugs. Studies also showed that most people with OCD require high doses of these drugs for them to be effective.

HOW THESE MEDICINES WORK

It still remains unclear as to how these medicines help in treating OCD. However, what we do know is that each of these drugs affects the production of serotonin, a chemical found in the brain. Serotonin acts as the messenger of the brain. This is to say that if the brain lacks in serotonin, it would not work right. Patients with OCD who have taken these drugs were helped by boosting their serotonin, causing their brain to be back on the right track.

Just like any other drug for a certain illness, these drugs have one or more side effects for most patients of OCD. As such, it is important for both the health professional and the patient to determine the benefits of the drug versus the side effects. In addition, patients with OCD should make sure to relay any problems that might be caused by the drug to the health professional. More often than not, if an OCD patient encounters problems caused by the drug, the health professional adjusts the dose or change the schedule of drug intake.

WHO CAN TAKE THESE MEDICINES

On the other hand, not all OCD patients can take these drugs. For instance, pregnant women especially those who are breastfeeding should avoid taking any drug for that matter. However, for pregnant women with severe cases of OCD, these drugs are proven to be safe as long as the dosage in controlled. Most women who are pregnant and suffering from OCD have taken them without experiencing any difficulty. Conversely, some pregnant women with OCD make use of Exposure and Response Prevention (ERP) to reduce taking medicines during their first or last trimester.

Although Anafranil is the first drug to be tested for OCD, very elderly patients should avoid it because of its side effects, most of which can hinder with the way they think. In some cases, the drug can cause confusion or worsen it. Similarly, OCD patients who have heart problems should take extra caution when taking Anfranil.

WHEN TO TAKE THESE MEDICINES

One of the most common mistakes of many OCD patients is

that they only take these drugs when they feel stressed out. For these medicines to work, they should be taken daily given that they do not work the same as typical anti-anxiety drugs. Anti-anxiety drugs are only taken when patients are anxious or upset. OCD patients should make sure they do not miss taking these medicines. On the other hand, doctors prescribe missed doses to OCD patients to help in managing side effects.

HOW OCD PATIENTS PERCEIVE TAKING MEDICINES

In general, patients with OCD think they have failed due to needing a medicine to help them. Mental health professionals try to help patients cope with such thought by letting them compare their illness with another medical disorder such as diabetes. It should be noted that OCD, apart from being a brain disorder, is also a medical illness. Thus, as a diabetic needs insulin to be able to face a normal life, OCD patients need medicines in order to go on with their lives as normally as possible.

On the other hand, a child with OCD may have various responses to these medicines. It should be noted that no two children are alike in the way they respond. Generally, Anafranil is not given to children due to its side effects. Thus, parents or guardians of a child with OCD should take note of factors that may guid the choice of medicine to use. These include potential side effects, positive response to a specific drug by other members of the family, cost or availability, and presence of other disorders.

HOW LONG WILL IT TAKE FOR THESE MEDICINES TO WORK

When doctors prescribe these medicines to be taken for just 10 to 12 weeks, it is important for the OCD patient not to give up before the medication even gets a chance to work. More often than not, patients have the tendency to believe that nothing is happening to them in the first weeks of taking the drugs; however, gradually, patients will soon notice a great improvement with the way they think and respond to their thoughts.

One of the most common problems when using medicines solely for OCD treatment is that the patient may not be aware if the drug is helping them specifically when not undergoing CBT. Although some OCD patients respond positively to medicine without CBT, most patients are required to take these drugs while undergoing CBT or ERP.

If a patient is having a hard time accepting that he/she needs a medicine to treat his/her OCD, it would help to think that medicines help correct neurological or chemical problem in the brain. However, if the patient needs CBT to help treat OCD or correct behaviors, it would help to think that the treatment would be faster if medicines are combined with behavioral therapy.

In most cases, mental health professionals recommend the use of CBT or ERP with the combination of medicines or just CBT. This is because the chances of good response for this type of treatment is maximized. Fortunately, most patients who are recommended with this type of treatment agree with the approach.

Thus, the most effective treatment or approach as

determined by many mental health professionals and psychiatrists, consists of CBT/ERP with the combination of medicines.

HOW THESE MEDICINES CAN BE OBTAINED

More often than not, OCD patients find it difficult to sustain their medicines due to its cost or price. For patients who cannot afford buying these medicines, some drug companies provide doctors and health care professionals free samples of these medicines. In turn, the samples are given by the doctor to their patients who cannot afford the costs. In addition, many drug companies extend programs to help patients obtain these medicines at a discounted price. In fact, some drug companies have programs that offer free medicines for patients who cannot afford the cost.

EXPOSURE AND RESPONSE PREVENTION (ERP) THERAPY

For many years, traditional psychotherapy, better known as talk therapy, has attempted to ameliorate a psychological condition through helping patients build an insight into their mental problems. However, for individuals with OCD, it is best to try cognitive therapy (CBT) first even though talk therapy may be beneficial as some point to an individual's recovery. This is because CBT is a type of treatment that has been proven to be the most effective in treating OCD.

CBT is composed of a large group of therapy strategies and the most important of all these strategies for OCD is referred to as the Exposure and Response Prevention (ERP).

Exposure is determined as the stage where the patient confronts his/her images, thoughts, situations, and objects, which causes anxiety. Many patients claim that they have tried confronting or facing thoughts and situations over and over again and still feel anxious in the end. Although most OCD patients may think that the concept of exposure is incorrect, it is necessary to take note that a second part is needed for the entire treatment to work. This part is referred to as Response Prevention.

As soon as an OCD patient faces his/her thoughts, situations, and images among others that cause anxiety, he/she should decide not to do compulsive behavior. This may sound a little incorrect for most OCD patients given that they may have tried stopping their compulsive behavior yet still end up anxious. On the other hand, an OCD patient should not be discouraged. Instead, he/she should continue making a commitment to discard compulsive behavior until such time that anxiety is reduced. It is very ideal for an OCD patient to stay committed to not giving in to compulsive behavior.

Once an OCD patient notices a significant drop in his/her anxiety, it means he/she stayed "exposed" to his/her thoughts and situations that cause him/her to be anxious. More so, the patient also "prevented" compulsive response, which is referred to as habituation. In most cases, the idea of ERP may be new for an OCD patient as his/her anxiety starts to drop just by staying exposed to the things that he/she fears and yet do not give in to compulsive behavior.

EFFICIENCY OF OCD TREATMENTS

As discussed previously, the best treatment for patients with OCD should be able to include at least one of the following: A cognitive behavior therapy (CBT) intervention referred to as Exposure and Response Prevention, medicines, family support and education, and a properly trained mental health professional.

Based on recent studies, an estimated 70% of individuals with OCD would be treated by CBT or medicine. In general, patients who respond to CBT report a maximum of 80% reduction in their OCD symptoms. On the other hand, patients who respond to medicines report a maximum of 60% reduction in their symptoms.

Conversely, for medicines to be efficient in treating OCD, patients should take them on a regular basis as well as participate actively in CBT.

Regrettably, at least 25% of patients with OCD were found to refuse treatment by CBT and as many as half of patients refuse or discontinue taking medicines for OCD due to side effects. Unfortunately, some patients find the medications unaffordable.

COMMON HINDRANCES TO EFFECTIVE TREATMENT

According to several studies, at an average, it takes 14 to 17 years for individuals with OCD to get proper treatment. This length of time includes the time the disorder begins. In general, this is how long an OCD patient gets effective treatment due to several hindrances or obstacles.

For one, some individuals with OCD prefer to hide their symptoms due fear of stigma or embarrassment. As such, most people with OCD choose not to seek any help from health professionals until the onset of symptoms becomes apparent after many years.

Another hindrance is that there was inadequate public awareness about OCD; thus, many people were unaware that the symptoms they have are associated with an illness that could undergo treatment.

Until recently, there was also lack of proper training in some mental health professionals, which leads to incorrect or inappropriate diagnosis. Some individuals with OCD symptoms who seek the help of several doctors spend years undergoing treatment; however, they are under wrong diagnosis.

You should take note that some therapists are trained better and have more efficient skills in treating OCD than others. When looking for a therapist, OCD patients should first ask for an interview to gauge the therapist's knowledge about appropriate OCD treatments. You should make sure that your therapist is adept to doing the ERP. A therapist's responses to your questions will determine whether he/she is the best for you. If you notice that the therapist is quite guarded, becomes angry at your questioning or withholds information, it is best to find another one. On the other hand, if the therapist is cordial enough to answer your questions and appreciates the importance of you making a decision, then you find the right one. It is important that your therapist is open, knowledgeable, and friendly given that you will be spending much time with him/her.

Apart from lack of proper training by some mental health

professionals, individuals with OCD have a hard time finding local therapists to treat their OCD symptoms effectively. Furthermore, if ever they find a local therapist, some OCD patients are not able to afford the treatment they need.

CHECKLIST IN SEARCH FOR THE RIGHT OCD THERAPIST

It is very important that you find the right therapist to help you treat your OCD. Here is a simple checklist that you can use to guide you in your search for the perfect OCD therapits.

First, ask the potential therapist about the techniques that can be used to treat OCD. If the therapist is hesistant, vague, or does not discuss cognitive behavior therapy (CBT) or exposure and response prevention (ERP), take caution at once.

Second, ask the potential therapist if exposure and response prevention (ERP) is used for treating OCD. If the therapist says that he/she uses CBT but is not providing specific details, be cautious.

Third, ask the potential therapist about his/her training, background, and experience in treating OCD. Take note if he/she tells about going to a CBT psychology graduate program or had a post-doctoral fellowship in CBT. Furthermore, take note if the therapist claims of being a member of the Association for Behavioral and Cognitive Therapies (ABCT) or the International OCD Foundation (OCDF). These are all good signs. It may also be a good sign if the therapist mentions his/her attendance in specialized trainings or workshops conducted by the ABCT or OCDF.

Fourth, ask the potential therapist about his/her attitude toward the use of drugs or medicines in treating OCD. It is a bad sign if the therapist is against, tentative, or negative about the efficiency of medicines for treating OCD.

Fifth, ask the potential therapist if he/she is willing to leave his/her clinic or office in case he/she does behavioral therapy. This is because in some cases, it is necessary to conduct exposure and response prevention (ERP) away from the clinic or office. If the therapist contradicts this, then you just found another bad sign.

Other pertinent questions that you might ask the potential therapist is the length of his/her practice involving anxiety disorders; the length of his/her practice involving individuals with OCD; and if he/she feels that he/she has been effective in treating patients with OCD.

Through this simple checklist, you will be able to find the best therapist that you need in order to treat your OCD appropriately and efficiently. As mentioned earlier, one of the hindrances OCD patients encounter on their way to recovery is ending up with a mental health professional who lacks knowledge and skills in OCD treatment.

Chapter 5 – In-Depth OCD Diagnosis

As mentioned in the previous chapters, OCD can be very common both in adults and children; however, it is often left undiagnosed. OCD can only be diagnosed by doctors, specialists, and trained therapists.

In general, diagnosis of OCD are based on three factors: the individual has obsessions; the individual has compulsive behaviors; and the obsessions and compulsions hinder the individual from doing important duties and activities such as going to school and working among others.

Obsessions are referred to as images, impulses, and/or thoughts, which transpire repeatedly, making the individual out of control. Obsessions can be disturbing given that they are often senseless. Thus, they are unwanted by a person as they can cause him/her to experience various feelings including doubt, disgust, fear, and/or a feeling of "over-righteousness." Obsessions can get in the way of an individual's important activities including attending to family duties and responsibilities, going to work/school, and socializing.

On the other hand, some people mistake obsessions for something they are not. For instance, it is normal for a person to have occasional images of getting sick or occasional thoughts about his/her loved ones' safety.

Some of the most common obsessions in OCD include contamination, losing control, perfectionism, harm, unwanted sexual thoughts, and religious obsessions among others.

Contamination may involve household chemicals, body fluids, dirt, environmental contaminants, and germs/diseases.

Losing control may involve a fear of acting on impulse to harm others, fear of swearing or yelling insults, fear of acting on the impulse to harm oneself, fear of stealing things, and fear of horrific or violent images in the individual's mind.

Perfectionism may involve fear of losing things, concern about exactness or evenness, fear of forgetting or losing significant information when throwing things, concern with a need to remember or know, and unable to decide whether to keep or throw things.

Harm may involve fear of harming others due to carelessness and fear of being responsible for a terrible incident.

Unwanted sexual thoughts may involve perverse or forbidden sexual impulses about other people, perverse or forbidden sexual images or thoughts, obsessions about aggressive sexual behavior towards other people, and sexual obsessions involving incest or children.

Religious obsessions, also referred to as scrupulosity, may involve excessive concern with morality or right or wrong and concern with blasphemy or offending God.

Other obsessions may include superstitious thoughts or ideas about certain colors and lucky or unlucky numbers and concern with acquiring a disease or illness not by contamination such as cancer.

Meanwhile, compulsions are behaviors or thoughts, which an individual gets into repeatedly in order to counteract, neutralize, or discard their obsessions. More often than not, individuals with OCD are aware that these compulsions are only temporary solutions to discarding their obsessions; however, they tend to rely on their compulsions when they are not provided with other ways to escape or cope. Like obsessions, compulsions can also get in the way of an individual's normal activities.

Conversely, when an individual experiences repetitive behaviors or thoughts, it does not necessarily mean they are compulsions. Religious practices, bedtime routines, and learning new skills may involve repetitive activities but are normal and part of daily life. In addition, an individual's behavior can be determined as compulsion if, say, he/she arranges books for several hours when he/she does not work in a library or bookstore.

Some of the most common compulsions in OCD include washing and cleaning, checking, repeating, and mental compulsions among others.

Washing and cleaning may involve excessive bathing, grooming, showering, toilet routines, and tooth brushing; excessive washing of hands or in a specific method; doing other things in order to prevent or discard contact with contaminants; excessive cleaning household stuff or other objects.

Checking may involve checking whether the individual harmed or will not harm himself/herself, checking if the individual has not done a mistake, checking that the individual did not or will not harm others, checking that nothing terrible transpired, and checking parts of physical body or condition.

Repeating may involve repeating routine activities like

getting up or down from the stairs or going in or out doors, rewriting or rereading, repeating activities excessively such as doing a task five times because 5 is a safe or right number, and repeating body movements such as blinking, tapping, or touching.

Mental compulsions may involve praying to prevent harm to others or oneself, mental review of events to prevent harm to others or oneself, undoing or cancelling out something such as a bad word with a good word and counting while doing a task until the end to reach a safe or right number.

Other compulsions include telling, confessing, or asking for reassurance, hoarding or collecting things or items resulting to excessive clutter, avoiding situations that may trigger obsessions, and putting things in order until it feels correct, safe, or right.

Chapter 6 – Tools for Managing OCD at Home

In order to manage OCD effectively, it is best to start building tools that include strategies, which can help you in dealing with your obsessions.

However, you need to know the vicious cycle of OCD in order to come up with the right strategies. The OCD cycle begins with the trigger, followed by the obsession, and then you come up with the meaning of your obsession, and ends in anxiety.

On the other hand, you can start breaking this cycle by learning to eliminate or discard unhelpful coping strategies gradually. Unhelpful coping strategies include compulsions. Next, you should learn to balance your obsessions.

There are several tools that you can use in order to break the vicious cycle of OCD.

TOOL 1: FACE YOUR FEARS – EXPOSURE AND RESPONSE PREVENTION (ERP)

One of the most efficient ways to break the cycle of OCD is to face your fears gradually. The technique that is used for facing fears is referred to as exposure and response prevention (ERP).

ERP is carried out through exposure to situations that bring on your triggers or obsessions. It is also done by not getting involved in unhelpful coping strategies such as avoidance and compulsions.

First, in order to face your fear through ERP, you should learn more about your OCD. You should be able to determine your obsessions and identify the triggers that result to your compulsions and obsessions. This can be done by keeping track of your triggers daily for at least a week.

Given that your obsessions can transpire frequently, you can write down 3 triggers a day, which will provide you an overview of your obsessions and compulsions. You can put labels to columns so you could rate the intensity of your trigger in a given situation. For instance, a column can be labeled as "fear" and rate its intensity ranging from 0 for no fear and 10 for extreme fear. You can then record your compulsions or other coping strategies to address an obsession. Make sure that you include both mental and/or behavioral strategies that you use in order to manage your obsession.

Second, you can make use of ERP to face your fears by building a "fear ladder." Once you have reached a week of tracking your obsessions and compulsions, you can make a list of all situations that you fear. You can then build a fear ladder by ranking your triggers based on their intensity, say, from least to most scary.

Take for example the fear of contamination. If you have fears of contamination, it is possible that the intensity is only 1 out of 10 when you are in a friend's house as compared to using the public restroom in a shopping mall. You may find that using a public restroom translates to a very high intensity of 9 out 10 on your fear ladder.

When building your fear ladder, it is best to separate a ladder for every obsessive fear you have. For instance, you may need a ladder for all related situations to your fear of contamination and another ladder for your fear of causing a terrible event to transpire.

Third, you can make use of ERP by climbing your fear ladder once you have built it. This is the stage where you are ready to face your fears through allowing yourself to be placed in situations that trigger your obsessions, which is exposure while resisting doing anything to control your obsessions along with the anxiety that comes with them, which is response prevention. You need not worry if you feel anxious as you try these drills. It only means that you are doing the right thing.

Facing Fears through Exposure

As you face your fears through exposure, start with the easiest item on your fear ladder and increase the difficulty as you go along. Make sure to track your progress, specifically your level of anxiety, throughout the exposure drill. This would allow you to determine the decline of your fear on a specific situation.

When doing the exposure drill, make sure not to avoid your fears. For instance, do not allow yourself to make subtle avoidance by touching the doorknob with just one finger instead of using your entire hand; talking to someone; or thinking about other things. When you engage in avoidance, it would be more difficult to face and get over your fears.

Take your time as you try to expose yourself to your fears. Make sure not to rush when you are in a specific situation until such time that your fear declines by at least a half. In addition, focus on facing and overcoming the first item on your fear ladder prior to moving on to another. Do the exposure repeatedly for the first item until it no longer becomes a problem or hindrance for you.

Doing the Response Prevention

Exposure would only work if you try to resist engaging into your compulsions. This means you have to resist your urge during or after the exposure. It is important to take note that the objective of ERP is to be able to face your fears without carrying out your compulsions.

Meanwhile, it can be hard for you to determine a way to face a specific situation if you have been giving in to your compulsions for quite some time. As such, it is best to ask the help of a family member or someone close to you without OCD. Ask them to model their behavior, say, leaving home without having to recheck appliances over and over or washing their hands as quickly as possible. This way, you may be able to adapt what their behavior.

If you are facing your fears for the first time, it can be difficult to resist a compulsion completely, but you can delay and reduce your rituals. Instead of not doing the compulsion entirely, you can at least delay acting upon it. For instance, if you entered a public restroom (exposure), wait for at least 10 minutes before leaving. If you touched something that you think is contaminated, wait for at least 5 minutes before you wash your hands and do it for a minute rather than 3 minutes. It would be very helpful if you try your best to prolong the delay until such time that you are able to resist your compulsion totally.

In the event that you find yourself carrying out a compulsion, it would be best to re-expose yourself immediately to that same situation that you fear. If you have to repeat re-exposing yourself, do so until such time that your fear drops altogether. Say, if you entered a public restroom, stay there for at least 5 minutes. Leave and re-enter the restroom and stay for another 5 minutes before leaving. Do this repeatedly until your fear drops by a half.

If you experience only a little anxiety as you complete a drill, it is time to move on to the next item on your fear ladder. For instance, if you feel just a little anxiety when entering a public restroom and staying there for 5 minutes or more; challenge yourself constantly. Stay inside the restroom for as long as you can handle and leave. Do this challenge repeatedly until your anxiety goes away entirely.

Tool 2: CHALLENGE AND REPLACE UNHELPFUL INTERPRETATIONS OF OBSESSIONS

This tool can be very efficient when combined with Exposure and Response Prevention (ERP) in order to address your disturbing thoughts, which are all part of OCD.

Even for people without OCD, it is normal to have unpleasant or unwanted thoughts once in a while. Some may be very much affected or bothered by such thoughts while others may not. When you are bothered by an unpleasant or unwanted thought, it is because of the interpretation or meaning that you associate with it. Individuals with OCD have the tendency to perceive unpleasant or unwanted thoughts as important, dangerous, and meaningful while those without OCD may simply

41

discard or bash the thought.

Take for example thinking that you might contract a serious disease because you touched something inside a public bathroom. For people who do not have OCD, they may simply find it weird for having such thought. Thus, they would not feel anxious and go on with their day.

However, if you have OCD, you automatically assume that it is highly possible for you to contract a serious disease when entering a public bathroom and touching something in it. You may even think that you can pass on the disease to your loved ones. Thus, this can make you very anxious, which leads you to giving in to a compulsion and starting the vicious cycle of OCD.

Consequently, it is vital to challenge unhelpful interpretations of your obsessions and replace them with helpful ones in order to manage OCD. As mentioned earlier, this tool can be very effective when combined with ERP.

How to Challenge Unhelpful Interpretations of Obsessions

There are 2 steps in order to challenge unhelpful interpretations of obsessions. These include knowing what you are thinking and managing your obsessions.

First Step: The first step involves knowing the interpretations you give to your obsessions prior to challenging them. You can start by tracking your obsessions and the interpretations or meanings you give to them. It is best to track them every day for at least a week. Keep track of at least three obsessions daily to provide you with a good overview of your pattern of thinking.

Record the situation that triggers your obsession under the "situation" column; obsessive thoughts in a specific situation under the "obsession" column; and all emotions you had as the obsession transpired under the "feelings" column. Make sure to rate the intensity of your feelings ranging from 0, which translates no emotion to 10, which translates to most intense emotion. Record your interpretations or meanings to your obsessions under the "interpretation" column.

You can determine the interpretations or meanings of your obsessions by asking yourself four basic questions. First, what the cause might be for you to be upset about a specific obsession. Second, what such obsession say about your personality or yourself. Third, what might be the kind of person you are if you did not have such obsession. Finally, ask yourself what might happen if you did not do anything about your obsession.

Second Step: The second step involves managing your obsessions once you are able to determine them as well as the manner of interpreting them. There are several sub-steps that you can do in order to manage your obsessions.

Sub-step 1: Learning the facts

It is normal to have unwanted or unpleasant thoughts although they can be annoying. However, these thoughts are harmless. Even if you have a specific thought, it does not mean it makes you a bad person or that it would come true. It is best to learn the facts about your thoughts and keep in mind that they are harmless unless acted upon.

Sub-step 2: Realistic Thinking

More often than not, adults with OCD have the tendency to fall into thinking traps just like others with another type of anxiety order. These thinking traps are often negative and unhelpful when it comes to looking at things. Thus, it is important to learn how to think realistically. This means that you have to look at all aspects of a specific situation including its positive, negative, and neutral aspects prior to making any conclusion. It is like looking at yourself and the world in a fair and balanced way.

Sub-step 3: Challenging Unhelpful Interpretations Of Obsessions Through General Strategies

In order for you to end up with a balanced way of perceiving your obsessions, ask yourself several pertinent questions:

Question 1: *What are the pros and cons of your type of thinking?*

Question 2: *Are your interpretations about a certain situation realistic or accurate?*

Question 3: *What evidence is for and against a specific interpretation?*

Question 4: *Have you mistaken a thought for a fact?*

Question 5: *Are you 100% certain that your thought will transpire?*

Question 6: *Is your judgment based on your feelings instead of reality or facts?*

Question 7: *Are you confusing certainty with possibility?*

Question 8: *Is there a more rational way of perceiving such situation?*

Once you are able to challenge your initial interpretation, you would be able to provide a balanced meaning to your obsession and replace them with calming and realistic ones. You would also find that challenging your interpretations can make you feel better. Although it may be difficult at first, you should not be discouraged. It is normal and expected to find it hard to believe the helpful interpretations you end up with at first; however, with constant practice, it will get much easier. You will soon find that your new interpretations are stronger than what you previously had.

Sub-step 4: Challenging Unhelpful Interpretations Of Obsessions Through Specific Strategies

There are several specific strategies that you can do in order to challenge some of the most common misinterpretations of obsessions. These include calculating the chances of danger, creating a responsibility pie, carrying out the continuum technique, and doing the survey method.

The method of calculating the chances of danger can help you be more realistic about the probability of your worst fear to happen. You should keep in mind that having a thought that something might happen does not mean it is true. It is important that you take note of your thoughts and determine if your OCD thoughts are unhelpful or wrong.

The responsibility pie can help you challenge excessive sense of responsibility that you may have. You can start creating your responsibility pie by writing down how responsible you would feel in the event that something you fear happens. Then, write all possible factors, which may contribute to such fear to happen. Create a circle and mark all pieces of the pie based on the percentage you think should be provided to each factor. Finally, draw and mark the percentage that you are responsible for. Determine if this percentage is relevant to your initial prediction.

The continuum technique can help you construct a better perspective of how you fair for having a "bad" or unpleasant thought. What you can do is to challenge such thought. Say, you have a very bad thought of running over an individual. You can make a list of people who might fit both ends of a continuum. You can label them as the gentlest person and most violent person.

After which, identify yourself in the continuum you made. Determine where you fit on it. Chances are, you may find yourself under the "most violent person." Conversely, as you try to think of people who have done violent acts instead of thoughts, you might re-think and change where you fit in the continuum.

Through the continuum technique, you might realize that you are being too hard on yourself. For instance, you might discover that having violent thoughts is better than acting on them. Eventually, you will be able to acknowledge that it is all right to have a bad thought as long as you do not act on them as compared to other people who commit violent acts.

Finally, the survey method can help you in challenging yourself about the need for certainty. You can do this by carrying out a survey among your family and friends about how well they do on the tasks they have or how they remember things that they read. Whatever you want to survey, compare the results with your initial predictions.

TOOL 3: MANAGING STRESS

Given that managing OCD is not an easy task, you may find that your progress would not be as good as expected. In addition, it is highly possible that your OCD can be more compelling whenever you undergo stress. As such, it is best to create a list of stressful situations that can possibly worsen your OCD. You should be able to anticipate what might cause your stress so in the event that it happens, you are prepared. You need to be proactive in reducing your stress through living a healthy lifestyle.

When managing OCD, it is important that you are brave enough to face everything that is associated with it. Once you notice any improvement, make sure to allot time to reward or give yourself credit.

Any progress you make should be followed up by practice. When you keep on practicing the drills and skills of managing OCD, you will soon realize that your obsessive fears have weakened.

Chapter 7 – Relationships and OCD

More often than not, when a member of a family is diagnosed with OCD, other members would surely ask how they could be able to help. There are several efficient steps that families and friends can help a person with OCD.

First, families and friends need to educate themselves about OCD. They can do this by reading books on OCD; attending support groups dedicated to OCD; joining OCD foundations; and researching online among others. Families and friends should be able to realize that the more they learn about OCD, the more they can help their loved ones with the disorder.

Second, it is necessary for families and friends to acknowledge and reduce behaviors of family accommodation. These behaviors are associated with things that families do, which trigger symptoms of OCD. While it is true that OCD demands affect families, friends, and other relationships constantly, it is how they respond that possible sparks off OCD symptoms. Once families and friends learn the proper responses and impact of their behaviors to a loved one inflicted with OCD, they would be empowered to create stability among them.

Third, families and friends can help a loved one with OCD find the right treatment for the disorder. Although medicines and cognitive behavior therapy are considered the most efficient treatments, family support and education is likewise a significant key to treat OCD.

Fourth, families and friends can learn how they can respond appropriately to a loved one with OCD who refuses

48

treatment. This can be done by offering encouragement to the individual. Say, families and friends can tell the individual that proper treatment causes a significant decrease in OCD symptoms. In addition, they can also tell the individual that there are others who are experiencing the same endeavor as theirs and that there is help. Offering encouragement may also include suggesting to the individual to attend support groups, speak to a professional in OCD, or talk to another OCD patient through online OCD foundations or support groups.

Families and friends can respond appropriately to an OCD patient by attending support groups where they can learn how to deal with the symptoms. They can also obtain feedbacks and other pertinent information from other families who also have an OCD patient.

Another way of responding appropriately to an OCD patient is *bringing materials with OCD information and leave it where the patient can read or listen on his/her own.* These materials may include video tapes, books, and audio tapes among others.

Finally, one of the most efficient ways to respond appropriately to a loved one with OCD is to *obtain support and help.* It is best for families and friends to seek the support or advice of a professional in OCD cases. Speaking with other families who are undergoing the same problem can also help family members and friends to release whatever they feel about the OCD patient.

PROBLEMATIC BEHAVIORS, RELATIONSHIPS, AND OCD

There are several problematic behaviors among families, friends, and other relationships that can affect a loved one with OCD. These include making changes in family routine; participating in a certain behavior; taking extra responsibilities; assisting in avoiding; making changes on a job; helping in a certain behavior; and making changes in leisure activities.

When it comes to making changes in family routine, this means that you can affect the behavior of a loved one with OCD by changing, say, the frequency of changing your clothes or changing the time that your shower in a day.

Participating in a certain behavior means that you go along with the OCD behavior of a loved one instead of correcting it. For instance, when the person suffering from OCD washes his/her hand, join in and wash your hands as well.

Taking on extra responsibilities means you go out of your way to take them somewhere whereas they are very capable of driving themselves to their desired destination.

Assisting in avoiding means that you tend to help your loved one with OCD avoid things that distract, disappoint, stress, or upset them. For example, it is possible to you try to wash their clothes for them thinking that you would be able to do it the right or proper way.

Making changes on your job means that you try to reduce your work hours so that you would be able to take care of your loved one with OCD.

Helping manage the OCD behavior of your loved one means

you "tolerate" the behavior. For instance, if your loved one is fond of buying cleaning products, you buy for them in large amounts.

Finally, making changes in leisure activities means that it is all right for you not to leave the house unless you are with your loved one with OCD. Thus, apart from tolerating the behavior, you also let the behavior affect your time with friends, interests in movies, or dining out.

Conclusion

Thank you again for purchasing this book!

I hope this book was able to help you to better understand what it means and feels like to have obsessive compulsive disorder and how to be successful in treating the disorder.

The next step is to apply what you have learned in this book to be able to get the full benefit of the information discussed within. Indeed, obsessive compulsive disorder is debilitating and difficult to live with. However, it is not impossible to overcome.

There are many ways for you to cope if you are suffering from obsessive compulsive disorder and you are not alone in this battle. If it is any of your loved ones who have obsessive compulsive disorder, especially if they are young ones, your support and patience will be greatly appreciated and will be astoundingly helpful as they go about recovery and treatment.

Although obsessive compulsive disorder cannot be permanently cured, there are many things that a sufferer can do to live a happy and normal life. Additionally, the patience and love provided by highly supportive family members, relatives, and friends will prove priceless.

Finally, if you enjoyed this book, please take the time to share your thoughts and post a review on Amazon. We do our best to reach out to readers and provide the best value we can. Your positive review will help us achieve that. It'd be greatly appreciated!

Thank you and good luck!

Check Out My Other Books

Below you'll find some of my other popular books that are popular on Amazon and Kindle as well. Simply click on the links below to check them out. Alternatively, you can visit my author page on Amazon to see other work done by me.

Cure For Controlling People: The Ultimate Guide for Releasing You from Those That Control You In A Relationship

http://www.amazon.com/Cure-Controlling-People-Relationship-Codependency-ebook/dp/B00JOHTV5K

ADHD Symptom and Strategies: The Ultimate Guide for Understanding and Handling Attention Deficit Disorder in Adults and Children

http://www.amazon.com/ADHD-Symptom-Strategies-Understanding-Hyperactivity-ebook/dp/B00JOZT3DM

Narcissism Unleashed 2nd Edition! The Ultimate Guide to Understanding the Mind of a Narcissist, Sociopath and Psychopath!

http://www.amazon.com/Narcissism-Understanding-Narcissist-Narcissistic-Personality-ebook/dp/B00JP0UQM8

How to Cure the Workaholic Addiction: Control Anxiety and Stress Before It's Too Late!

http://www.amazon.com/How-Cure-Workaholic-Addiction-Workaholics-ebook/dp/B00JPZJY2Q/

Living with Autism: The Successful Steps to Recognizing, Adapting, Learning, and Understanding Autism

http://www.amazon.com/Living-Autism-Recognizing-Understanding-Breakthrough-ebook/dp/B00JQS6Z5Q

The Ultimate Self Esteem Guide: Steps to Building Self Esteem, Confidence, and Inner strength!

http://www.amazon.com/Ultimate-Self-Esteem-Guide-Codependancy-ebook/dp/B00JY2F3K2

The Shopping Addiction: A Cure for Compulsive Shopping and Spending to Free Yourself from Addiction!

http://www.amazon.com/Shopping-Addiction-Compulsive-Self-Help-Impulsive-ebook/dp/B00JY2FYDS

Living With OCD: A Powerful Guide To Understanding Obsessive Compulsive Disorder In Children And Adults

http://www.amazon.com/Living-OCD-Understanding-Compulsive-Personality-ebook/dp/B00K3E3E06

BOX SET #1: Narcissism Unleashed! & Cure For Controlling People

http://www.amazon.com/BOX-SET-Controlling-Narcissistic-Codependency-ebook/dp/B00KAATSFI

BOX SET #2: Narcissism Unleashed! & Mind Control Mastery

http://www.amazon.com/BOX-SET-Narcissistic-Personality-Manifestation-ebook/dp/B00K9URU90

BOX SET #3 ADHD Symptoms & Strategies & Living With OCD

http://www.amazon.com/Symptoms-Strategies-Attention-attention-hyperactivity-ebook/dp/B00KA0K4SI

BOX SET #4: Living With OCD & The Ultimate Self Esteem Guide

http://www.amazon.com/BOX-SET-Ultimate-Confidence-Strength-ebook/dp/B00KA0U04G

BOX SET #5: Narcissism Unleashed! & Mind Control Mastery & The Shopping Addiction & Living With OCD & The Ultimate Self Esteem Guide

http://www.amazon.com/Box-Set-Narcissism-Compulsive-Psychopath-ebook/dp/B00KK96T56

If the links do not work, for whatever reason, you can simply search for these titles on the Amazon website to find them.

CPSIA information can be obtained
at www.ICGtesting.com
Printed in the USA
LVHW081120090119
603245LV00021BA/1067/P